C

Morality

Carla E. Fritsch
William J. Raddell, Jr.

The Center for Learning

The Publishing Team

Rose Schaffer, HM, M.A.,
President/Chief Executive Officer

Bernadette Vetter, HM, M.A., Vice President

Mary Anne Kovacs, M.A., Editor

William J. Raddell, Jr., M.P.S., Content Editor

Cover Design

Susan Sheaffer Curtis, B.A.

Nihil Obstat

The Reverend John J. Blazek, CSC
Censor Deputatis

Imprimatur

The Most Reverend Anthony M. Pilla, D.D., M.A.
Bishop of Cleveland

Given at Cleveland, Ohio on 7 April 2000.

The *Nihil Obstat* and *Imprimatur* are official declarations that a book or pamphlet is free of doctrinal or moral error. No implication is contained therein that those who have granted the *Nihil Obstat* and *Imprimatur* agree with the contents, opinions, or statements expressed.

ISBN 1–56077–519-X

Contents

Page

Preface v

The Authors vii

A Conversation Starter viii

Definitions 1

Morality 1

Catholic Morality 2

Moral Determinants 5

Morality: A Call to Holiness 6

Virtue 6

Freedom 7

Love 8

Society and Morality 9

Contemporary Attitudes 9

Morality and Culture 11

Social Morality 12

The Hebrew Scriptures 14

Covenant 14

The Law 14

The Ten Commandments 15

Christian Scriptures 17

The Call to the Kingdom 17

Discipleship 18

The Beatitudes 19

Moral Teaching and Church Authority 21

The Magisterium 21

Papal Infallibility 22

A Positive Approach 23

Kohlberg's Stages of Moral Reasoning 23

Fundamental Option 28

Striking a Balance 29

Conscience **30**
Definition 30
Functions of Conscience 31
Formed Conscience 31
Conscience and Civil Authority 33
Sin **35**
Biblical Concepts 35
Commission and Omission 36
Original Sin 36
Reconciliation 37
The Sacrament of Reconciliation 38
Grace **40**
Definition 40
God's Love 40
Bibliography **41**

Preface

Throughout Christian history, living a moral life has been considered a key component of living a Christian life. A problem, however, is that there are many ways to approach morality and a diversity of opinions as to what is in fact moral. Even among followers of Jesus disagreement exists. The Catholic Church teaches that there is a best and most faithful way to interpret and apply the teaching of the Judeo-Christian tradition to our lives. The goals of this book are to describe the Catholic approach to morality, to contextualize it within a committed relationship to Jesus Christ, and to invite a deeper response to God's calling to become a holy people.

Catholic Teaching is a series intended for adults interested in updating their own understanding of current Catholic theology and the application of those theological insights to their own life circumstances. This series aims to help the individual become more literate about the Catholic tradition, to appreciate the richness and breadth of Catholic thought, and to aid in the processes of religious formation and ownership of one's faith experience. Many adults have a desire to learn more about the Catholic faith tradition, yet because of the demands of daily living have little time to pursue additional education. The Catholic Teaching series has been developed to help those individuals by giving a concise overview of mainstream Catholic thought on a variety of topics important to the life of the Church.

Each book provides a conversation starter to stimulate reflection on an issue dealt with in the text, basic background information on the topic, and reflection questions to help readers recognize and integrate these elements into their spiritual life. These questions are interspersed within the text at the conclusion of major topic headings. It is recommended that the conversation starter and reflection questions be read prior to reading the text. Upon completion of one's reading, return to the conversation starter and reflection questions in light of ideas surfaced in contemplation of topic coverage.

The Authors

Carla E. Fritsch, who earned her M.A. at John Carroll University, Cleveland, Ohio, is a religion teacher and theology department chairperson. She has served as coauthor and editor of various curriculum units in The Center for Learning's Faith and Novel/ Drama series.

William J. Raddell, Jr., who earned his Masters in Pastoral Studies at Loyola University of Chicago, is a religion teacher and theology department chairperson. He has served as an author and a series director for The Center for Learning's Discipleship series and Theological Perspectives series.

A Conversation Starter

One area of great controversy today is the issue of abortion. The pro-life movement asserts that abortion is objectively wrong and that few, if any, circumstances would allow an individual to elect to take the life of an innocent preborn child. This position is espoused by the Catholic Church, as well as by evangelical and fundamental Christian denominations. Protection of the unborn has been a cause which has united these churches, and they have been vocal about seeking an end to legalized abortion. One Christian based pro-life group, Operation Rescue, has even gone to the point of performing acts of civil disobedience, blocking access to abortion clinics in an attempt to save the lives of the unborn and to dissuade women from having abortions.

Those who support legalized abortion claim that a woman has a right to choose to have an abortion and that no group, civil or religious, has the right to limit this option. They state that religious bodies have no right to impose their morality upon society. Pro-choice adherents maintain that the individual alone can determine what is moral for him/her, and, therefore, no one has the right to restrict another's choice.

- If this reasoning were applied to other issues, would it be possible to have a system of law?
- Are there standards which apply to all persons everywhere?
- If morality is subjective and based on an individual's personal feelings and perspectives, can any individual or group condemn the moral choices of another?

- Can something be legal and yet immoral? Conversely, can something be moral and yet illegal?
- The Right to Life Society has avoided the position of addressing abortion as a moral issue and instead addresses it as a civil rights issue, claiming that abortion deprives an unborn child of the most basic human right, the right to life. Does such an approach sidestep the issue of morality?

Definitions

Morality

Morality involves an understanding of human behavior in terms of right and wrong. The term *moral* refers to that which is good, a life-giving response to a moral decision. To be moral is to act virtuously. *Immoral* refers to that which is evil, a life-denying response, not acting in conformity with accepted principles of right and wrong. An amoral action is one which is morally neutral; it is neither good nor bad. The term *amoral* can also be used to refer to a person who lacks moral standards, who has no concept of right and wrong.

A common obstacle in understanding morality is the notion that what one group considers immoral, another may accept as moral. There is a relative character of human behavior, since morality varies from one culture to the next. However, every culture has taboos, laws, and controls that limit human behavior. Such laws are considered absolute and inviolate. Most of these standards preexist Judeo-Christian morality. **Natural law** thus shows the way to a higher order but is always interpreted within a cultural context.

Natural law—basic and universal concepts of right and wrong

Regardless of an individual's cultural background or faith system, certain principles of ethical behavior can be considered to be absolute. Rather than being defined by social norms, the values of dignity, fairness, honesty, and integrity are universal to the human experience. These principles are termed *natural law* because their origins are derived from human nature itself.

Catholic Morality

Moral systems are rooted in natural law. Various systems seek to interpret human actions in the light of some ultimate meaning. Christian morality can be defined as behavior based on one's relationship to Jesus Christ. Christian morality seeks to guide individual and communal behavior on the basis of Jesus' teachings and lifestyle, which transcend the dictates of natural law. In other words, Christian morality defines the values of dignity, fairness, honesty, and integrity (i.e., the principles of natural law) in light of the teachings and lifestyle of Jesus Christ.

Christian morality is diverse; there are many valid ways to approach it. All Christian traditions seek to be faithful to Jesus' mandate to love, Catholic morality is a particular tradition or understanding as to how this may best be lived out. Catholicism has a distinctive approach. Though a number of the elements that distinguish this approach are shared by other Christian faiths, it is the way these are combined that makes them recognizably Catholic. Catholic morality seeks to interpret the Christian experience through both Scripture and Tradition (i.e., teachings of the Church Fathers, conciliar pronouncements, and **Magisterium**. Catholic morality incorporates the duties incumbent upon members of the Roman Catholic community. It is not intended to replace Christian morality, but to particularize Christian concepts within a Catholic context.

Magisterium—official teaching authority of the Church shared by the pope and bishops

In reality, Catholic and Christian morality were synonymous until the time of the Reformation. Protestant reformers replaced Catholic preaching (Tradition) and confessional practice with scriptural mandates for behavior. Troubled consciences were resolved in the Protestant system through the justification of faith alone. Note, however, that the twenty-one Church councils almost never dealt with questions of morality, and there has never been an infallible papal pronouncement in the area of morality. Moral teaching developed primarily through the consensus of theologians. Starting in the nineteenth century, when the pope began to emerge as Catholicism's supreme moral theologian, a specifically identifiable body of Catholic teaching arose in the forms of papal encyclicals and bishops' pastoral letters. Aimed at all people, not just Catholics, this body of teaching addresses both personal and social morality.

The principle of *sola scriptura* (Scripture alone) was adopted by many Protestant sects. This concept states that the Bible alone contains all of the moral guidance necessary for salvation. Catholicism has always taught that, while Scripture is the primary source for moral direction, natural law and Tradition are also means of God's revelation.

The Catholic approach likewise differs from the Protestant view that, as a result of the fall, human nature lost its original state of goodness and the world became a place of evil. The Catholic tradition sees humanity as flawed, yet still good, and the world also as a place of good. It recognizes that truth can come from a variety of sources, even those not expressly Christian. It enters into a dialogue with culture, joining with it to promote the common good, appropriating what is of value, and criticizing anything that harms human dignity and welfare.

The Church sees morality not as merely a matter of individual interpretation, but as rooted in a rich, two-thousand-year history of shared wisdom as to how best to interpret and apply Jesus' teaching in order to live out the moral demands of the Gospel.

In its emphasis on formed conscience as the highest moral authority, Catholicism recognizes that there are objective and subjective dimensions to moral decision making. Catholics acknowledge the importance of being informed and guided by Scripture and by the Tradition of the Church, but also recognize that the individual has the responsibility to grapple with the question of how best to apply moral principles revealed by those sources to specific situations in the spirit of love. This is attested to in the *Catechism of the Catholic Church*:

> Conscience enables one to assume *responsibility* for the acts performed. If man commits evil, the just judgment of conscience can remain within him as the witness to the universal truth of the good, at the same time as the evil of his particular choice. The verdict of the judgment of conscience remains a pledge of hope and mercy. In attesting to the fault committed, it calls to mind the forgiveness that must be asked, the good that must still be practiced, and the virtue that must be constantly cultivated with the grace of God:
>
>> We shall . . . reassure our hearts before him whenever our hearts condemn us; for God is greater than our hearts, and he knows everything.* [1781]

The *Catechism* views morality (see paragraphs 1715, 1718) as a means of enhancing the dignity of all persons and as God's guidance to help us to achieve ultimate happiness, rather than simply as adherence to rules and regulations. Morality is a pathway to the fulfillment of Jesus' statement, "I came so that they might have life and have it more abundantly" *(John 10:10)*. The Church sees morality as an element of an integrated reality along with creed, worship, and prayer. This perspective has led to the strong emphasis on the social dimension of morality.

* *1 Jn 3:19–20*

The Catholic Church also teaches that the faithful themselves have a sense or instinct about what is good and true. The Second Vatican Council specifically mentions this gift of the Holy Spirit which enables the Church to achieve universal agreement in matters of faith and morals *(Dogmatic Constitution on the Church,* 12). This charism insures that moral directives are not haphazardly imposed from the top, but are inherent in the dignity of human beings.

Moral Determinants

In order to judge the goodness or badness of an action, Catholics are called to look upon the actions of Jesus Christ as the hallmark of perfection. Three guidelines exist to help us evaluate our actions. First, the nature of the act itself is examined. It can be measured against a set of objective norms. Second, the situation surrounding the act is examined to determine any mitigating circumstances. Third, the intention behind the act is also examined. A moral determination is made, therefore, by examining the totality of an act: its purpose, its precipitating circumstances, and its motivation.

There are many who would say that there is no such thing as a moral standard which applies to everyone. They believe that morality is a subjective reality which each person must determine individually.

How can you know what is truly right and good? Why do you choose to be moral?

Morality: A Call to Holiness

Christians believe human destiny is the unification of the person with God in heaven, a sharing in the divine life. Implicit in this vocation is the call to holiness, to become increasingly Christlike. Saint Paul speaks of the necessity of becoming a "new creation." This call to "Be holy because I [am] holy" (*1 Peter 1:16*) originates in God and occurs in union with God. Each person is called out of brokenness and inauthentic existence to develop full potential as the person God created him/her to be. Holiness is a call to wholeness, which can happen only through a continuing process of conversion, the surrender of the human will to the divine will. This occurs through making moral choices. Moral actions lead an individual toward his or her ultimate destiny; immoral actions detract from that destiny. This is not to say that humans can earn or merit heaven. Rather, moral actions flow from our relationship to God and from our human nature. See the *Catechism of the Catholic Church,* paragraphs 2012–2016, 2030.

Virtue

Theological virtues—faith, hope, love

Cardinal virtues—prudence, justice, fortitude, temperance

In response to the call to holiness each person is called to develop virtue in his/her life. A virtue is a habit of doing good. Virtues enable us to live in a manner consistent with the kingdom of God. They guide human conduct, directing us toward God and ultimate happiness and away from self-centeredness. The result is a strengthening of the individual's relationship with God, others, and self.

Development of virtue requires effort. It starts with the desire to respond to God's love and a willingness to surrender to the Holy Spirit in order to be transformed into the very image of God. Virtues are acquired and deepened through practice, but aided by God's grace. They are the evidence of God's activity in a person's life and the fruit of a life committed to God's purpose. Catholics believe that sacraments lead and aid us in living virtuously.

For more information about virtue, see the *Catechism of the Catholic Church*, paragraphs 1803–1845.

Freedom

Freedom is the philosophical basis of American society. Our culture places great emphasis on personal freedom, which is often equated with unrestricted choice. In the Judeo-Christian tradition, however, freedom is a gift, the purpose of which is that we may seek the Creator and respond to the divine invitation to love.

Free will—ability to choose to do God's will

Central to this understanding of freedom is the doctrine of **free will**. Free will essentially refers to one basic choice—whether to do our will or surrender to God's will. We are free to choose or reject relationship with God. That choice will then influence all subsequent choices. Because of this, freedom is a basic human right, an essential part of human dignity.

Morality is a response to God's invitation to an eternal relationship which can only happen through a free and unconditional response, since Christ desires us to be free from sin and free to enter into the kingdom of God. Disobedience to God's will by choosing evil is a misuse of freedom and leads to the slavery of sin and the possibility of excluding ourselves from God's kingdom. Choosing to do good, however, brings the individual even greater freedom, which must be exercised with the knowledge that we are responsible for our choices and actions. Morally, freedom is limited by concern for the common good and by the need for public order. See the *Catechism of the Catholic Church,* paragraphs 1730–1749.

Do you tend to see morality as a restriction of personal freedom or as a means of achieving greater freedom?

Love

The primary motivation for choosing to be moral is love. It is also the standard for moral behavior, the ultimate arbiter of what is moral. Love is the nature of God and participation in the life of God. When Jesus identified the supreme commandment as the imperative to love God and love one's neighbor (*Matthew 22: 37–40*) he identified the way we are to respond to God's love and enter into the kingdom of heaven. Since our ultimate destiny is the kingdom of love, we must invest ourselves in that kingdom.

Agape—a Greek term for love; considered the highest form of love

This love is the building block of community. It is best understood in the Greek concept of **agape**, a form of love which is unselfish, unconditional, and always concerned with the best interest of the other. Thus human existence finds its meaning in loving relationships. The failure to love harms the community and one's relationship with God; therefore morality always seeks to guide the individual to the most loving thing to do in each particular circumstance. See the *Catechism of the Catholic Church,* paragraphs 1822–1829.

How do you discern the most loving thing to do when you face a moral dilemma?

Society and Morality

Contemporary Attitudes

Prior to the seventeenth century, life and reality were viewed from a realistic or pragmatic perspective based on Greek philosophy and culture. This outlook believed that deeper truths could be reached by reflecting upon the visible world. The light of reason, accompanied by God's grace, could lead to an understanding of the underlying sacred reality revealed in the natural order. Saint Thomas Aquinas used this system of thought in his theological writings.

During the seventeenth century, when science influenced the Enlightenment, the primary way of understanding reality shifted from objective truth to empiricism. Only that which could be measured or verified could be considered real. Truth became equated with fact. This mind-set introduced subjectivism, skepticism, individualism, and relativism into the contemporary thought process. These called into question whether there can be common values and absolute truths that apply to all persons; they led to the idea that each individual must determine what is true for oneself. In his encyclical, *Evangelium Vitae* (The Gospel of Life), Pope John Paul II points out that technical and scientific thinking rejects "the very idea that there is a truth of creation which must be acknowledged, or a plan of God for life which must be respected."[1]

[1]John Paul II, *Evangelium Vitae* (Washington, D.C.: United States Catholic Conference, 1995), 40.

As a consequence of this shift, contemporary culture is characterized by attitudes such as, "It's your opinion against my opinion; there is no absolute truth." This is reflected in the moral dimension. Each person becomes the sole arbiter of what is moral; moral choices are a personal matter; an individual's personal feelings and perspectives are the ultimate standard for behavior. Nowhere is this more evident than in the rallying cries of supporters of legalized abortion: "It's my right to choose!" and "You have no right to impose your morality upon me."

These assertions deny the reality stated in the *Catechism of the Catholic Church.*

> The Old Testament attests that *God is the source of all truth.* His Word is truth. His Law is truth. His "faithfulness endures to all generations."* Since God is "true," the members of his people are called to live in the truth.** [2465]

In *Evangelium Vitae*, Pope John Paul II identifies the effects of this denial. "The eclipse of the sense of God and of man inevitably leads to a *practical materialism* which breeds individualism, utilitarianism and hedonism."[2]

To combat this contemporary mentality, the Church, particularly in book three of the *Catechism,* responds in a countercultural way and boldly states that it has a vision of God and the divine plan for humanity, the social order, and ultimate truth. It is in this context that the Church can make the claim to be the authentic moral teacher as it transmits the revealed Word of God.

**Ps 119:90;* cf. *Prov 8:7; 2 Sam 7:28; Ps 119:142; Lk 1:50.*

***Rom 3:4;* cf. *Ps 119:30.*

[2]John Paul II, *Evangelium Vitae*, 40.

Morality and Culture

Some people hold that the moral teachings of the Scriptures may have been appropriate for the period in which they were written, but today are outdated and need to be revised in consideration of modern cultural norms. The fallacy of such an argument is that it fails to recognize that while behavior may vary with cultural standards, human nature does not. This is not to say that there are not moral laws which were culturally conditioned, e.g., Jewish dietary laws. Such a position, however, overlooks the fact that there are values which are universal to all humanity. Certain principles of moral behavior can be considered absolute and therefore not dependent on a particular cultural background. Reason, natural law, and Church teaching all address a universal understanding of good characterized by honesty, fairness, integrity and protection of the innocent.

Throughout Christian history morality has been countercultural. The Church has consistently upheld values of societal responsibility, the common good, and personal accountability. It is difficult to recognize immorality when it has widespread cultural acceptance. This is readily seen in today's society in issues such as materialism, sexual promiscuity, and abortion. In such a milieu, the Church seeks to sensitize society to those values and moral principles long held by human society and espoused in the gospel. Christians are to influence the culture rather than the reverse.

How has contemporary culture influenced your understanding of morality?

Consider ways you have been desensitized by cultural practices.

What experiences raised your consciousness and helped you to look as these practices from a gospel perspective?

Social Morality

The Judeo-Christian tradition has always recognized that morality has both personal and social dimensions. In the Scriptures the implied answer to Cain's question, "Am I my brother's keeper?" (*Genesis 4:9*), is a resounding yes. Nowhere is this more clearly stated than in the description of the judgment of the nations in the twenty-fifth chapter of Matthew's Gospel. The first pastoral issue addressed by the early Christian community entailed caring for widows and orphans.

This social dimension, however, goes beyond the demands of charity. It is difficult to read the Psalms without finding some reference to a call for justice. The prophets frequently echoed the notion that justice is an integral component of what God requires of humanity. Jesus' command to love also entails working for justice. His Jerusalem ministry shifted from the focus on meeting individual needs that typified his Galilean ministry to addressing unjust attitudes and practices within institutional religion.

Central to Christian understanding are the beliefs that all persons are endowed by God with dignity and fundamental human rights, and that each individual has an eternal destiny with God. The U.S. Bishops' pastoral, *Justice in the World (Justitia in Mundo, 1971)*, states that work for justice is a constitutive element of preaching the Gospel. In its commission to evangelize and through its participation in the prophetic ministry of Jesus, the Church is called to work actively toward the transformation of society. We recall this each time we pray the Lord's prayer: "Your kingdom come on earth as it is in heaven." In the encyclical *Evangelium Vitae*, Pope John Paul II states:

> It is therefore a service of love which we are all committed to ensure to our neighbor, that his or her life may be always defended and promoted, especially when it is weak or threatened. It is not only a personal but a social concern which we must all foster: concern to make unconditional respect for human life the foundation of a renewed society.[3]

Under the subheading, "the political community and the Church," the *Catechism of the Catholic Church* states:

> It is a part of the Church's mission "to pass moral judgments even in matters related to politics, whenever the fundamental rights of man or the salvation of souls requires it. The means, the only means, she may use are those which are in accord with the Gospel and the welfare of all men according to the diversity of times and circumstances* [2246].

[3]John Paul II, *Evangelium Vitae*, 140.

*GS 76 § 5.

The Hebrew Scriptures

The Hebrew Scriptures are the initial stage of ongoing revelation. They represent the revelation of God, the divine will, and the desire that humanity live in loving relationships with God. They represent a valid and continuing revelation of God. Rather than being made obsolete by the Christian Scriptures, they are necessary to understand Jesus and his moral teaching, which is rooted in Hebrew faith. However, the expressions of truth they contain must be interpreted in light of the gospel.

Covenant

Covenant—permanently binding love commitment

Central to the Hebrew Scriptures is the concept of **covenant**. Grounded in Abraham's relationship to Yahweh, and ratified through Moses during the Exodus, the Covenant established Israel as God's Chosen People. Significantly more than a contract, a covenant establishes a blood relationship between a greater and a lesser party. Israel's Covenant originated in the God who acted in history to save the people. Its stipulations were born out of gratitude for God's loving kindness expressed from the beginning of time. The Covenant called the people to live up to the honor of being God's chosen ones.

The Law

The Law, or Torah, disclosed God's will and was the mechanism through which the people remained faithful to the Covenant previously established through God's saving power. Rather than inhibiting, the law was considered to be life-giving. Through adherence to its dictates, the people found a sense of common identity and direction for their lives. God's care and concern for them as a people was not conditional upon their following the Law. God's love was (and is) unconditional.

Jesus made clear that his purpose was to fulfill the Law. His focus, however, was on the spirit rather than the letter of the law. The *Catechism of the Catholic Church* gives us a clear perspective from which to understand the law:

- It prepares us to understand the gospel.
- It is fulfilled, clarified, and surpassed by the gospel.
- It is brought to perfection by the gospel.

The Ten Commandments

The Ten Commandments or Decalogue (literally the *ten words*) were always linked to the Covenant. Adherence to the Commandments was a way of showing fidelity to God. They form the starting point or center for the rest of the law. The Commandments protect human dignity and conserve basic values of society. Disobedience harms the community. Though a prohibitive form of morality, they outline acceptable behavior, giving an exact description of the individual's duty. Although similar in content to pagan laws, the Ten Commandments are unique because they originated with God rather than with human beings. They were seen as a means to help people become what God called them to be.

1. I, the LORD, am your God, . . . You shall not have other gods besides me.
2. You shall not take the name of the LORD your God in vain.
3. Take care to keep holy the sabbath day.
4. Honor your father and your mother.
5. You shall not kill.
6. You shall not commit adultery.
7. You shall not steal.
8. You shall not bear dishonest witness against your neighbor.
9. You shall not covet your neighbor's wife.
10. You shall not covet your neighbor's [goods].

Jesus reveals the full meaning of the Commandments. Today Christians view them as a basic or minimal standard, since Jesus calls us far beyond the avoidance of doing evil to live out an active love. The commentary on the Commandments composes a major portion of Part III: Life of Christ in the *Catechism*. This section expands on a contemporary understanding of the moral implications of the Commandments in light of the imperatives of the gospel.

Christian Scriptures

The Call to the Kingdom

The Christian Scriptures echo Jesus' call to participate in the kingdom of God. At the heart of the message is the necessity of repentance. John the Baptist, Jesus, and the early Church all preached repentance as a key condition for entry into the kingdom of God. True repentance was more than mere sorrow for sin. The believer was called to a change in conviction as well as in practice (*Luke 3:10–14*). This **metanoia** involved a reorientation of life. An individual was called to make God the center, to place God's will foremost in life.

Metanoia—change of heart, conversion

The Christian was called to repent and believe. This belief in Jesus as the Christ was to raise the Christian to a new level of consciousness—Kingdom consciousness. This conversion experience was to be ongoing. Through belief in Jesus and adherence to the will of God, Christians were to be transformed into the image of God. Jesus' ministry proved that living in the light of God's love enables one to be good. The conversions of Zacchaeus and Mary Magdalene illustrate this truth.

Participation in the kingdom of God expands our vision beyond the limitations of human experience. Reality is understood as more than just the physical world experienced through the senses. It involves a spiritual dimension. Only when, through faith, we accept God's invitation to a relationship, can we discern this spiritual reality. When Jesus promised his disciples that he would send the Advocate, he told them, "But when he comes, the Spirit of truth, he will guide you to all truth" (*John 16:13*). In John's account of Jesus healing the blind man, the man did not just receive his eyesight; he also received spiritual sight which allowed him to see spiritual truths.

These spiritual truths are revealed to humanity by God through the Scriptures. God's will is most completely and compellingly seen in the teaching and example of Jesus. Saint Paul reminds Timothy, "From infancy you have known [the] sacred scriptures, which are capable of giving you wisdom for salvation through faith in Christ Jesus. All scripture is inspired by God and is useful for teaching, for refutation, for correction, and for training in righteousness, so that one who belongs to God may be competent, equipped for every good work" (*2 Timothy 3:15–17*). The Scriptures provide a basic understanding of God's will which is the basis for Catholic morality.

There are Christian denominations who consider actions like gambling, drinking alcoholic beverages, smoking cigarettes, dancing, and going to the movies to be sinful.

Why do these groups consider these things to be sinful while the Catholic Church does not condemn these practices?

Discipleship

When Jesus walked the earth, he invited his disciples; "Come, and you will see." *John 1:39* implies that the invitation was a call to live the life Jesus lived. Those who are Christian are called to live a particular style of life. To be a disciple means to imitate Christ. Discipleship is the heart of Catholic morality. Rather than living according to a codified rule of life, Christians are to seek to incarnate the Christ by allowing the Holy Spirit to transform them into his image.

The life Jesus lived was an embodiment of the greatest commandment. Jesus said, "You shall love the Lord, your God, with all your heart, with all your soul, and with all your mind. This is the greatest and the first commandment. The second is like it: You shall love your neighbor as yourself. The whole law and the prophets depend on these two commandments" (*Matthew 22:37–40*).

The Law and the revelation of the prophets were derived from this two-part commandment, Jesus was the living manifestation of this commandment. Likewise, his disciples were to reflect this same life of love. Rather than reducing the law to a set of rules and regulations, Jesus expanded it to a way of life. This way of life is the essence of Catholic morality.

In what ways is the notion of discipleship as the heart of Catholic morality different from an understanding of morality as adherence to moral laws?

The Beatitudes

The Sermon on the Mount is a discourse that describes a style of life for Jesus' disciples. The author of Matthew's Gospel set this discourse on a mountain with the intention of drawing a parallel between God giving the Law to Moses on Mt. Sinai and Jesus describing a way of life to his disciples. The teaching describes what love of God and neighbor entail for the disciple of Jesus. The Beatitudes describe the happiness a Christian can experience by living according to the teaching and example of Jesus. Both Matthew's and Luke's accounts of this discourse describe Catholic Morality as living by the dictates of the kingdom rather than by a set of rules and regulations.

Blessed are the poor in spirit,
for theirs is the kingdom of heaven.

Blessed are they who mourn,
for they will be comforted.

Blessed are the meek,
for they will inherit the land.

Blessed are they who hunger and thirst for righteousness,
for they will be satisfied.

Blessed are the merciful,
for they will be shown mercy.

Blessed are the clean of heart,
for they will see God.

Blessed are the peacemakers,
for they will be called children of God.

Blessed are they who are persecuted for the sake of righteousness,
for theirs is the kingdom of heaven.

Blessed are you when they insult you and persecute you and utter every kind of evil against you [falsely] because of me. Rejoice and be glad, for your reward will be great in heaven.

—Matthew 5:3–12

To what extent are you familiar with the moral teaching of the Hebrew and Christian Scriptures?

When examining your conscience, which do you find to be a more helpful guide—the Ten Commandments or the Beatitudes?

Moral Teaching and Church Authority

The role of Church authorities in moral matters is not the exercise of power but one of service. The concern of the Church is the proclamation of the reign of God and the salvation of souls. In its exercise of authority, the purpose is not to control but to help those entrusted to its care to find authentic freedom. The Judeo-Christian tradition has always maintained that humanity is dependent upon God's revelation to know what is truly good; therefore, Scripture is the primary source of moral understanding.

The Church helps us to interpret the moral teaching of Jesus and apply it to our lives. The pope and bishops guide the faithful on moral issues. This function is a gift of God for the building up of the Christian community.

> And he gave some as apostles, others as prophets, others as evangelists, others as pastors and teachers, to equip the holy ones for the work of ministry, for building up the body of Christ, until we all attain to the unity of faith and knowledge of the Son of God, to mature manhood, to the extent of the full stature of Christ, so that we may no longer be infants, tossed by waves and swept along by every wind of teaching arising from human trickery, from their cunning in the interests of deceitful scheming.
>
> —*Ephesians 4:11–14*

The Magisterium

Central to this function is the magisterium, which is the teaching authority of the Church. The magisterium is composed of the pope and bishops who have the responsibility of ensuring faithful adherence to the teaching of Jesus. They are aided by theologians who study, interpret, and articulate what God has revealed. Through the magisterium the Church is rooted in a two-thousand-year tradition of shared wisdom. This office is expressed in council decrees, synods of bishops, formulations of creeds, papal encyclicals, pastoral letters, and catechisms, a current example of which is the *Catechism of the Catholic Church* issued in 1994.

Papal Infallibility

Papal infallibility—a doctrine of the Church which states that the pope can speak without error in specific circumstances

Ex cathedra statement—an infallible statement

An example of God's continuing care and guidance for the Church is expressed in the doctrine of **papal infallibility**. This refers to the ability of the pope, in concert with the bishops of the Church, to speak in specific circumstances without error. This function can only be exercised in two areas—faith and morals—and then only when there is the intent to define a teaching of infallibility. Such pronouncements are exceedingly rare. This expression of Church authority has only been invoked twice since the doctrine was defined at the end of the nineteenth century. In each case the purpose was to bring clarity and provide authoritative teaching in response to questions about an area long a part of Church Tradition. When the pope chooses to speak infallibly he declares it to be an **ex cathedra statement** (literally, *from the chair)* referring to his authority as the one who sits on the throne of Peter to make such a statement on behalf of the Church. Such pronouncements are considered to be divinely revealed truth to be believed by all faithful Catholics. See the *Catechism of the Catholic Church,* paragraphs 888–892.

A Positive Approach

In *Leviticus 19:2*, God says, "Be holy, for I, the LORD, your God, am holy." God, who is holy, calls us to become like him. To be holy is to be whole, to become fully what God, our creator, intends us to be. Sin keeps us from becoming whole. The work of the Holy Spirit prompts us to live lives obedient to the will of the Father. It is helpful if we recognize that this is achieved through process.

Insight into human development, given to us by psychology, helps us recognize that there is a process involved in moral development. The stages include growth from self-centeredness to other-centeredness. The capacity to reason also grows from reliance on external authority to fidelity to internalized values. Catholic morality is best understood as that which draws us toward unconditional love, a love concerned solely with the well-being of the other.

Kohlberg's Stages of Moral Reasoning

Lawrence Kohlberg's theory of stages of moral reasoning offers a useful construct for discussing moral decision making. Kohlberg suggested that people understand moral reasoning at their own stage, at stages lower than theirs, and usually at the stage just above theirs. They find great difficulty in understanding moral reasoning at two or more stages above their own. Studies have also shown that people are attracted to the next higher stage, and that encountering moral dilemmas, whether real-life or hypothetical, facilitates growth.

Kohlberg's theory sees moral reasoning in three levels, each of which incorporates two stages:

Level One
The Pre-Conventional Level

Moral reasoning results from consequences of actions, such as punishment, reward, or exchange of favors, and from the physical power of authority figures.

Stage 1: Punishment and Obedience Orientation (ages 0–7)

Physical consequences determine whether an action is good or bad, regardless of its human meaning or value. Decisions at stage 1 are based on avoidance of punishment ("getting away with it") or earning rewards. "Good" behavior entails blind obedience to authority figures who have power over the person.

Stage 2: Personal Usefulness (ages 7–11)

Decisions are based on a desire to satisfy an individual's needs and occasionally the needs of others. Reciprocity, or mutual giving, is always for pragmatic reasons, with very little consideration of gratitude, justice, or loyalty. Reasoning is largely based on an attitude of "you scratch my back and I'll scratch yours."

Level Two—The Conventional Level

Moral reasoning involves maintaining the expectations of family, peer group, or nation for one's own sake regardless of the immediate consequences. A desire to respect, maintain, support, and justify the existing social order is found.

Stage 3: Conforming to the Will of the Group (ages 11–25)

People equate good behavior with whatever pleases or helps others. The person often conforms to the accepted or approved behavior of the majority. Behavior is often judged by the intention of the person ("he or she means well") regardless of actions. An individual earns approval and acceptance by being "nice."

Stage 4: Authority and Social Order, Law and Order (begins around age 15, increases to age 25)

Decisions result from a desire to uphold the existing authority, fixed rules, and social order for its own sake. Right behavior consists of doing one's duty, showing respect for authority, and "keeping things as they are."

Level Three—Post-Conventional Level

A person reasons according to moral values and principles that are valid and applicable apart from the authority of the group. Moral reasoning becomes more comprehensive, reflects universal principles, and is based on internalized norms.

Stage 5: Social Contract and Human Rights (can be reached beginning around ages 21–25)

Decisions result from critical examination and recognition of an individual's rights and standards agreed upon by a society within a social contract (such as the Declaration of Independence). The person's reasoning stresses the "legal point of view," but with an emphasis upon the possibility of changing laws when they fail to serve the welfare of society.

Stage 6: Universal Ethical Principles, Personal Conscience (can be reached beginning in the late 20s)

Decisions are based on a personal commitment to self-chosen universal ethical principles. Justice, equality of human rights, and the dignity of human beings as individual persons are recognized and respected because they are seen to be valid and necessary foundations. When any laws violate these principles, the person acts in accordance with the principles, no matter what the cost to self. The welfare of other persons is a supreme concern, regardless of who they are.[4]

Kohlberg holds that these stages are natural, not artificial or invented. They are also universal and sequential. An individual does not skip stages, but it is possible to slip back to a previous stage when under stress. One may experience more than one level at a time. In addition, a person may reason one way and act another. Usually, however, reasoning and behavior are closely related. An individual can become fixed at any level and may not reach mature morality. Some statistics indicate that fifteen percent to twenty percent of American adults continue to think at the pre-conventional level, most adults remain on a conventional level, and only about one-half of one percent of American adults reach the highest level.

Current research indicates a gender bias to Kohlberg's theory, which was developed after study of the male population. The works of Robert Staller, Nancy Chodorow, Carol Gilligan, and others point to significant differences between male and female moral development.

[4]Lawrence Kohlberg, "The Claim to Moral Adequacy of a Highest Stage of Moral Judgment," *The Journal of Philosophy*, 70 (October 25, 1973): 631–632.

Studies suggest that women tend to view their lives in terms of relationships that demand a sense of care and responsibility, and to approach moral dilemmas with the goal of solving conflicts. Feminine moral imperatives often emphasize alleviating trouble and making sure nobody gets hurt.

When viewed in terms of Kohlberg's stages, then, most women would place Stage 3 (Conforming to the Will of the Group) higher than Stage 4 (Authority and Social Order). Similarly, on the post-conventional level, the underlying truth is perceived differently by men and women. Men base moral judgments on principles of impartial justice, fairness, and equity. Women base moral judgments on principles of caring, nurturing, and responsibility.

Such distinctions in moral perceptions take on new dimensions when addressing the topic of social morality. A case in point is the concept of a preferential option for the poor, which teaches that the needs of the poor must take priority over the wants of the rich—even if the eradication of the problem is at great personal cost to the rich. Such a position may make no sense to an impartial justice mind-set, but it makes perfect sense to those who see it as the only way to solve the problem in a caring manner.

Remember that Kohlberg's Stages of Moral Reasoning are determined by a person's normative way of reasoning when making moral decisions rather than on actions.

Where would you place yourself in the stages? Why?

How has your understanding of conscience changed as you have matured?

Fundamental option—human freedom to choose for or against the kingdom of God

Fundamental Option

Fundamental option refers to the human freedom either to respond to or to reject Jesus' call to the kingdom. It is the choice of a direction or pattern for an individual's life. Freedom is usually thought of as something that applies to daily choices, but underlying all daily decisions is a more basic choice between selfishness and love, between self and God.

Automatic responses, like the many activities that occupy everyday life, are based on superficial levels of free choice. Fundamental option underlies all other choices. It inspires and supports everything one does or leaves undone. Acting according to this option, an individual approaches daily activities characterized by a more profound meaning and unity. Each person has a basic decision to make, to be a "giver" (as Jesus was), or a "getter." This fundamental stance can only be chosen gradually. The process of choosing it means coming to know oneself (including all personal limitations and possibilities).

Morality, then, is viewed in terms of this choice. To say no to God's invitation to the kingdom is to opt for selfishness, to choose personal will over the will of God. Individual selfish acts do not reverse a positive fundamental stance, but they may weaken it. Patterns of serious sin, however, over time and with consistency, could result in the rejection of God.

Would you say that your pattern of living clearly points to accepting God's invitation to the kingdom?

Striking a Balance

Approaches to morality vary greatly. There are those who perceive morality as a matter of conformity to preexisting norms. The fundamentalist Christian tradition takes such an approach. Morality is viewed as adherence to civil and religious law. Jesus' frustration with some of the Pharisees appears to have been caused by their rigid application of the Law without an emphasis on its value. At the other extreme are the people who maintain that there are no standards which can be applied to all situations. Rather, it is the situation that determines what is moral and what is not; there are no objective norms that can be depended upon to determine the morality of an act.

Catholic morality strikes a balance between these two extremes. Christian ethics contain an objective as well as a subjective dimension. For Christians, Jesus' teaching and example, as well as the truths contained in the Hebrew and Christian Scriptures, represent a norm that guides moral decision-making. Jesus offered a vision of life—the vision of the kingdom of God—to guide us in choosing a direction for our moral choices. He emphasized love as a standard for human behavior. Jesus told stories to illustrate the nature of that love instead of laying down a rule of life.

Rather than allowing personal circumstances to determine the morality of one's actions, Jesus taught that the individual must attempt to respond with love to all situations. Jesus avoided giving minimum and maximum standards for moral behavior. When Peter asked him how many times one must forgive, and when the teacher of the Law wanted Jesus to define who one's neighbor was, Jesus instead chose to present an ideal and allow them to decide. Catholic morality, then, acknowledges both the importance of norms for moral behavior and the responsibility to apply those norms to concrete life situations.

Conscience

Definition

Conscience—an action of the intellect that is applied to the evaluation of a moral decision

Conscience is not based on feelings, intuition, or will. It refers to an activity of the intellect in which reason is used to evaluate the rightness or wrongness of a specific action. Conscience involves both an objective and a subjective dimension.

Objectively, conscience applies knowledge to guide a person's understanding as to the morality of an action. Various influences provide input into what is right or wrong. Parents are typically the earliest influence. As an individual grows, family, friends, peers, the educational and legal systems, the media, and the individual's religious tradition are all sources of influence.

However, these impacts have different degrees of influence on each individual. In a society that espouses pluralistic values and moral relativism, these sources of moral knowledge may provide conflicting insights. The advice of peers may conflict with the advice of parents. The values of the media may contradict the values of one's religious tradition. The subjective dimension arises as value is assigned to the knowledge received. Cultural attitudes, beliefs, and practices strongly affect an individual's moral responses. It is sometimes difficult for Christians to recognize immorality in practices that are generally accepted by their own cultures. Society exerts strong positive effects when it reinforces values such as honesty, fidelity, and diligence. On the other hand, the task of developing a mature conscience is inhibited when society promotes self-indulgence, unstinted competition, and materialism.

Functions of Conscience

Three particular functions are performed by the conscience. The first is the establishment of a fundamental sense of value and personal responsibility. One must consider the relative importance of conflicting options. Second, one must judge the morality of a given action, as well as the consequences of acting or refusing to act. Finally, one must decide what is to be done in a specific situation. This choice involves the realization that the action may be wrong, but this is what should be done (to the best of one's understanding). Consider those situations (admittedly rare) when one must act, even when the consequence of such an action would be morally objectionable under other circumstances. For example, taking the life of another is wrong, but in the case of an ectopic pregnancy (the development of a fertilized ovum outside the uterus), taking the life of the unborn child would happen as a medical consequence of correcting an unnatural condition in the mother. If the condition remained uncorrected, neither the mother nor the child would live.

Formed Conscience

When we examine the notion of conscience from the perspective of Catholic morality, we recognize that there is another step that must be taken in the moral decision-making process. Since the various influences that communicate a sense of right and wrong are random and may vary greatly from individual to individual, it becomes the responsibility of the Christian to form his or her own conscience. Rather than leaving conclusions about value and personal responsibility to chance, the Christian must take deliberate action to ensure that his or her conscience will be a reliable guide for moral decision-making.

When making moral decisions, do you emphasize feelings or an informed conscience?

A conscience is formed by informing it. By seeking information and acknowledging that there are moral norms to guide Christian behavior, we attempt to develop a sound body of knowledge to aid in the decision-making process.

There are three primary areas that help to inform the Christian conscience. The first is the revelation of God found in the Scriptures. God continually reveals his will and an understanding of what is authentically good. This revelation finds its fullness in the teaching and example of Jesus. The second involves the teaching and Tradition of the Church as it attempts to understand God's revelation and apply it to the human experience. The Church possesses wisdom developed over a two-thousand-year period during which it has reflected upon its experience. The third area is to apply Jesus' command to love as a standard for moral behavior. The individual must consider what action love requires in any given situation. If the action is loving, then there is an obligation to act upon it. If it is unloving, then there is a need to refrain from it.

The Roman Catholic Church believes that a formed conscience is the highest authority in moral decision-making. It teaches that each person has both the right and the obligation to follow his or her conscience. It also recognizes that conscience must go beyond mere intellectual reasoning. Each person must be guided by faith, prayer, knowledge of God's will, and the power of the Spirit to make the best and most loving choices for all concerned.

Conscience and Civil Authority

In its discussion of the fourth commandment, the *Catechism of the Catholic Church* describes the duties of civil authorities and the duties of citizens in paragraphs 2234–2243. Since its inception, the Church has taught that Christians must be subordinate to civil authority, since all authority comes from God. In *Romans 13:1–7*, *1 Timothy 2:2*, and *1 Peter 2:13–17*, the Christian Scriptures teach that authority is given by God for the purposes of guaranteeing civil order, promoting the common good, insuring the fundamental rights of all persons, and dispensing justice. Resisting legitimate authority is seen as opposition to what God has ordained.

When, however, civil authority fails in its duties or conflicts with basic Christian principles and acts in a manner contrary to morality, Christians are under no obligation to obey. In such cases, civil decrees lack any binding force and the believer is obligated to follow the dictates of a well-formed conscience by refusing compliance, resisting unjust laws, and at times opposing them through **civil disobedience**. Biblical precedents can be found in the example of the Hebrew midwives and their refusal to kill all newborn Hebrew males (*Exodus 1:15–22*) and in the response of the apostles when ordered by Jewish authorities to cease preaching in the name of Jesus (*Acts 5:29*).

Civil disobedience—deliberately breaking the law, with a willingness to accept consequences, to point out the immorality of the law or to draw attention to injustice

This position is firmly stated in the *Catechism*:

> The citizen is obliged in conscience not to follow the directives of civil authorities when they are contrary to the demands of the moral order, to the fundamental rights of persons or the teachings of the Gospel. *Refusing obedience* to civil authorities, when their demands are contrary to those of an upright conscience, finds its justification in the distinction between serving God and serving the political community. "Render therefore to Caesar the things that are Caesar's, and to God the things that are God's."* "We must obey God rather than men** [2242].

Prior to the Vietnam War and the Watergate scandal, most Americans would have equated being a good Christian with being a good citizen. These two events led to a questioning of civil authority and questions about the morality of political decisions.

How can one determine if what is legal is moral?

This same questioning of authority has expanded beyond questioning civil authority to a suspicion of religious authority as well.

What contemporary examples do you see of this questioning of the Church's authority?

Since the Second Vatican Council, the Church has become increasingly vocal in its criticism of government policies and has addressed issues of justice which touch the political arena.

To what extent do you believe the Church should address issues in government and society?

**Mt 22:21*
***Acts 5:29*

Sin

Biblical Concepts

One of the Hebrew root words for sin literally means "to miss the mark." When we fail to orient ourselves toward God by turning away from the Commandments, Beatitudes, and teachings of Jesus, we misplace loyalty and "miss the mark."

The Hebrew Scriptures present sin as infidelity to the Covenant. By putting human interest before the will of God, the people divided their loyalty. It was as if they had stumbled on their faith journey, becoming waylaid with unimportant matters.

The Synoptic Gospels almost always connect sin to forgiveness. Jesus constantly reaffirmed God's love for humanity and showed that sin and human failings could be overcome through God's power. Jesus did not condemn sinners; he called them to return to a right relationship with God.

Perhaps the fullest theology of sin is found in the writings of Saint Paul. He wrote in the Epistle to the Romans that we cannot overcome sin through our own efforts, but only through the death and Resurrection of Jesus Christ who alone conquered sin and death. Paul commanded the Christian community to live in perfect imitation of Jesus Christ.

Sin can be understood as a failure to love God, self, or others. Most people tend to concentrate on isolated acts rather than attitudes of sinfulness that motivate the acts. Such attitudes of sinfulness (i.e., lovelessness, alienation, self-centeredness, and apathy) are the areas that need the healing light of forgiveness. "Surface" acts of sin are really symptoms of these deeper areas of brokenness within us.

Commission and Omission

Saint Augustine defined sin as "a word, deed, or desire in opposition to the eternal law." Such a definition links sin to a deliberate action that is unloving toward God, self, or others. Sin can also involve the absence of a loving action. Sin involves not only what we do (i.e., the commission of an act) but also what we fail to do (i.e., the omission of an act).

In what ways can sins of omission have even weightier and more far-reaching consequences than sins of commission?

Original Sin

Original sin—human beings are imperfect and are born into an imperfect world which has an effect upon their perception and actions

Original sin is often identified simply as an act of disobedience on the part of the first man and woman. If an individual goes no further in considering the meaning behind this act as it is recorded in Scripture, that person fails to see the reality of original sin as it influences personal relationships and decisions.

Basically, original sin is the imperfect, weak human nature that every individual possesses. The biblical author of Genesis, in writing the symbolic story of Adam and Eve, was suggesting that this unruliness must have been the experience of humanity from its beginning. Thus it is called "original."

Persons, individually and collectively, find that they are incapable of eliminating the effects of evil in their lives or in the course of history. Thus, they may feel caught by a situation that they cannot totally overcome alone.

The influence of a weakened situation created by original sin reveals itself in the difficulty of resisting the choice of self over others. Such a choice all too frequently profits self based on earthly standards. For example, greed, deceit, and war are commonly more profitable in terms of wealth, recognition, and power, than are self-sacrifice, honesty, and peace. One obvious proof of this is the amount of space devoted to reporting crime and corruption in daily newspapers.

Theologian Harvey Cox offers interesting insight into the Genesis story in his book *The Secular City: Secularization and Urbanization in Theological Perspective.* He suggests that the basic flaw in humanity is apathy, that is, the failure of individuals to take responsibility for the direction of their lives or the world.

Reconciliation

The social effect of sin deserves serious consideration because it can weaken and even destroy one's relationship with God and others. Continued willful, sinful actions are external signs of deeper attitudes of sin. Such actions cause an erosion process, wearing away the structure of Christian life. It is essential to remember that God's love and mercy are always available. God never deserts humanity. Jesus recognized sinfulness in the world, and he offered the Our Father, with its emphasis on forgiveness, as the perfect prayer.

Christians may often fail in love because of human weakness. This brokenness needs recognition, not as an excuse for our failings, but rather as an opportunity to seek the healing power of God. Once shortcomings are admitted, God's love, mercy, and healing can take place. Regardless of these failings, the Lord is always present. God wants all people to be whole and healthy in both personal and communal dimensions.

The gospels depict Jesus' forgiving attitude toward Mary Magdalene, Peter, the woman taken in adultery, and many others. He condemned only the smug and self-righteous. Jesus did not do away with the Law; he called Christians to live beyond the limits of law, to fulfill the promise of our potential. His call to a life of love involves truth, wisdom, humility, grace, and many risks.

Individual reconciliation with God, although good and necessary, is only part of the healing process. Individual sins weaken the entire Christian community. The community as a whole cannot reflect the Body of Christ if even one member ceases to live the Christian life. The Christian community, damaged by individual sin, also needs to be reconciled. It needs to celebrate God's love as it has been revealed in the forgiveness of Jesus Christ.

The Sacrament of Reconciliation

The Church recognized this need and with it the need for ongoing repentance and forgiveness. In baptism all previous sins were forgiven. This was ritualized in the practice of immersion which symbolized the process of dying to sin and rising to new life in Christ. The process of sanctification, though, was not complete; human nature had not been perfected, so the need for forgiveness continued to be a concern. This gave rise to the Sacrament of Reconciliation as a means of healing broken relationships, repairing the damage done by sin, and as an aid to growth in holiness.

Originally the community and later the priest as a representative of the community, commissioned by Jesus to forgive sins, aided the penitent in this process. The sacrament celebrates God's forgiveness, encourages and supports repentance, and guides the sinner toward reconciliation with God and neighbor as well as moral growth. In doing so it affirms the basic goodness of the sinner, addresses the communal as well as the individual dimensions of sin, and focuses on the grace and healing available from a loving God.

Grace

Definition

Any study of Catholic morality must be understood in the light of grace. Grace is the presence of God; it is the divine self-giving. Morality is best understood as a response to grace. Grace is a gift from God, offered to all. The Father seeks to gather humanity (*John 6:44*). However, the believer must respond to God's invitation by accepting Jesus' word and acting in accordance with it. This is the heart of Christian morality. To live morally is to live by grace. To live by grace is to acknowledge God dwelling with us. It is God who makes us good. Note here a difference between the Catholic perception outlined above and the Protestant understanding of grace supplanting human nature.

God's Love

Only grace can save. Without union with God, one cannot reach full personhood. Saint Paul states in the Epistle to the Romans that nothing can separate us from the love of God. Salvation is not a matter of worthiness; it is a gift. Humanity cannot earn salvation through simply acting in a moral manner. Morality is a pattern of acknowledging and living in accordance with that gift. In other words, we are called to live a moral lifestyle because we are saved. We do not live a moral life in order to be saved.

How have you experienced God's grace?

Bibliography

Baum, Robert, and James Randell, eds. *Ethical Arguments for Analysis*. New York: Holt, Rinehart, and Winston, 1973.

Bockle, Franz. *Fundamental Concepts of Moral Theology*. New York: Paulist Press, 1968.

———. *Fundamental Moral Theology*. New York: Pueblo Publishing, 1980.

Callahan, Sidney. *In Good Conscience: Reason and Emotion in Moral Decision Making*. San Francisco: Harper and Collins, 1991.

Catechism of the Catholic Church. Washington, D.C.: United States Catholic Conference; and Vatican City: Libreria Editrice Vaticana, 1994.

Cessario, Romanus, O.P. *The Moral Virtues and Theological Ethics*. South Bend: University of Notre Dame Press, 1991.

Cox, Harvey. *The Secular City: Secularization and Urbanization in Theologocal Perspective*. New York: Macmillan, 1966.

Curran, Charles E. *Themes in Fundamental Moral Theology*. Notre Dame: Fides, 1977.

Curran, Charles E., and Richard A. McCormick, S.J. *Readings in Moral Theology No. 7, Natural Law and Theology*. Mahwah, N.J.: Paulist Press, 1991.

Duska, Ronald, and Mariellen Whelan. *Moral Development: A Guide to Piaget and Kohlberg*. New York: Paulist, 1975.

Gilligan, Carol. *In a Different Voice: Psychological Theory and Women's Development*. Cambridge, Mass.: Harvard University Press, 1982.

Gula, Richard M. *What Are They Saying About Moral Norms?* New York: Paulist Press, 1982.

Haring, Bernard. *Free and Faithful in Christ*. New York: Seabury Press, 1978–1981 (2 vol.).

John Paul II. *Evangelium Vitae*. Washington, D.C.: United States Catholic Conference, 1995.

Kohlberg, Lawrence. "The Claim to Moral Adequacy of a Highest Stage of Moral Judgment." *The Journal of Philosophy* 70 (October 25, 1973): 631–632.

Maguire, Daniel. *The Moral Choice*. New York: Doubleday & Co., 1979.

McBrien, Richard P. *Catholicism*. Minneapolis: Winston Press, 1981.

McCormick, Richard. *Notes on Moral Theology, 1968–1980*. Washington, D.C.: University Press of America, 1981.

Overberg, Ken, SJ. *Conscience in Conflict: How to Make Moral Choices*. Cincinnati: Saint Anthony Messenger Press, 1990.

Schnakenburg, Rudolf. *Moral Teaching of the New Testament*. New York: Herder and Herder, 1964.

Smurl, James F. *Religious Ethics—A Systems Approach*. Englewood Cliffs, N.J.: Prentice Hall, Inc., 1972.

The Publisher

All instructional materials identified by the TAP® (Teachers/Authors/Publishers) trademark are developed by a national network of 460 teacher-authors, whose collective educational experience distinguishes the publishing objective of The Center for Learning, a nonprofit educational corporation founded in 1970.

Concentrating on values-related disciplines, the Center publishes humanities and religion curriculum units for use in public and private schools and other educational settings. Approximately 600 language arts, social studies, novel/drama, life issues, and faith publications are available.

Publications are regularly evaluated and updated to meet the changing and diverse needs of teachers and students. Teachers may offer suggestions for development of new publications or revisions of existing titles by contacting

The Center for Learning
Administration/Creative Development
P.O. Box 417, Evergreen Road
Villa Maria, PA 16155
(800) 767-9090 • FAX (724) 964-1802

The Center for Learning
Editorial/Prepress
24600 Detroit Road, Suite 201
Westlake, OH 44145
(440) 250-9341 • FAX (440) 250-9715

For a free catalog containing order and price information and a descriptive listing of titles, contact

The Center for Learning
Customer Service
P.O. Box 910, Evergreen Road
Villa Maria, PA 16155
(724) 964-8083 • (800) 767-9090
FAX (888) 767-8080
http://www.centerforlearning.org